# Francis Crick and James Watson: Pioneers in DNA Research

*John Bankston*

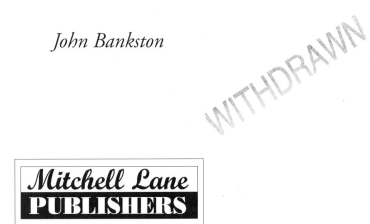

*Mitchell Lane*
**PUBLISHERS**

PO Box 619 • Bear, Delaware 19701
www.mitchelllane.com

# Unlocking the Secrets of Science

## Profiling 20th Century Achievers in Science, Medicine, and Technology

# Francis Crick and James Watson: Pioneers in DNA Research

Printing     1     2     3     4     5     6     7     8     9     10

Library of Congress Cataloging-in-Publication Data
Bankston, John, 1974-
    Francis Crick and James Watson: pioneers in DNA research/John Bankston.
       p. cm. — (Unlocking the Secrets of Science)
    Includes bibliographical references and index.
    Summary: Reviews the lives and accomplishments of Francis Crick and James Watson, who are credited with solving much of the mystery of heredity by mapping the structure of DNA.
    ISBN 1-58415-122-6
    1. Crick, Francis, 1916—Juvenile literature.  2. Watson, James D., 1928—Juvenile literature.  3. Geneticists—Biography—Juvenile literature. [1. Watson, James D., 1928- 2. Crick, Francis, 1916- 3. Molecular biologists. 4. DNA—Research.] I. Crick, Francis, 1916- II. Watson, James D., 1928- III. Title. IV. Series.
QH429.B36 2002
576.5'0092'2—dc21
                                                                        2002023655

**ABOUT THE AUTHOR:** Born in Boston, Massachusetts, John Bankston began publishing articles in newspapers and magazines while still a teenager. Since then, he has written over two hundred articles, and contributed chapters to books such as *Crimes of Passion* and *Death Row 2000*, which have been sold in bookstores around the world.  He has recently written a number of biographies for Mitchell Lane including books on Albert Einstein, Alexander Fleming, and Jonas Salk. He currently lives in Portland, Oregon.

**PHOTO CREDITS:** cover: Corbis; p. 6 Photo Researchers; p. 9 Corbis; p. 10 top and bottom: Cold Spring Harbor Laboratory (CSHL); p. 12, 13 CSHL; p. 16 Corbis; p. 18 left and right: Corbis; p. 20 CSHL; pp. 21, 22 Corbis; p. 28 top: Photo Researchers, bottom: CSHL; pp. 31, 33, 35 Corbis; p. 36 the Rockefeller University Archives; p. 38, 40 CSHL; p. 42 Corbis; pp. 46, 48, 49, 50 CSHL.

**PUBLISHER'S NOTE:** In selecting those persons to be profiled in this series, we first attempted to identify the most notable accomplishments of the 20th century in science, medicine, and technology. When we were done, we noted a serious deficiency in the inclusion of women. For the greater part of the 20th century science, medicine, and technology were male-dominated fields. In many cases, the contributions of women went unrecognized. Women have tried for years to be included in these areas, and in many cases, women worked side by side with men who took credit for their ideas and discoveries. Even as we move forward into the 21st century, we find women still sadly underrepresented. It is not an oversight, therefore, that we profiled mostly male achievers. Information simply does not exist to include a fair selection of women.

# Contents

*James Watson (left) and Francis Crick made unlikely partners when they first met as Crick was a middle-aged doctoral student and Watson was a young man in his early twenties who had already earned his Ph.D. Professionally, though, the two men complemented each other quite well. They both believed the study of genetics was the most important work a scientist could do. They met at Cambridge University's Cavendish Laboratory and quickly became great friends. Together, they set out to determine the structure of DNA and to build a three-dimensional solid model.*

# Chapter 1

## *Tiny People*

• • • • • • • • • • • • • • • • • • • • • • • • • • • • • • • • • • • • • •

**W**ho are you?

What color are your eyes, your hair, your skin? Do you have diabetes, fallen arches, mood swings? What person do people say you most resemble? Your mother? Your father? A great-grandfather who died 30 years before you were born?

The answers to these and many other riddles about life are the subject of genetics—the discipline that focuses on heredity and the desire to discover why every living thing develops a certain way.

The key to these secrets lies with deoxyribonucleic acid (DNA). Although this long, thin fiber was first identified in 1868, it took quite some time before its significance was understood. Many scientists called DNA a "stupid substance," believing it lacked a useful function.

They couldn't have been more wrong.

The twin strands of DNA, connected by a slight twist in the center, are organized into sections of genes. It is these genes that carry the instructions for making the proteins that comprise a cell. These proteins are responsible for what a cell does, what it looks like, how they are arranged. DNA isn't a "stupid substance" at all. Instead, it determines exactly what you look like, and some believe it has a great deal of influence in terms of who you are.

In many ways, the journey to the discovery of DNA's true function began with a Dutch lens crafter in the 16th century. His invention of a crude microscope about 1595 would enable scientists in the following century to form opinions about previously invisible organisms.

As microscopes improved, a scientist named Robert Hooke studied a piece of cork. Its enlarged image reminded him of the small rooms in monasteries where monks lived. These tiny spaces were called "cells" and Hooke gave that name to the minute structures he observed—structures that eventually would become recognized as the basic building blocks of all life.

Other scientists were convinced they'd solved the riddle about heredity when they saw what they believed were "homunculi," or tiny people, swimming inside the cells. Of course they didn't see tiny people at all. Instead their "visions" were a combination of poor magnification and good imagination.

It would take further improvements in microscopes, not to mention a number of scientific experiments, to prove there weren't tiny people swimming in cells. Even then, the question remained: What is responsible for an individual's inherited characteristics, that special blend of mother, father and every ancestor back through time?

It would take the work of two young men to solve the riddle. They constructed a model for the molecular structure of DNA that could be used to explain how living cells reproduce themselves in their own likeness. Their efforts helped to solve the puzzle of genetic inheritance.

The work of this pair, conducted in the middle of the 20th century, created a road map for scientists to use in the 21st. The reference work *Current Biography 1963* says of the two men's model, "In its fruitfulness for further discovery, [it] has been compared to Newton's laws of motion, Darwin's theory of evolution, and Einstein's relativity theories."

These two men were unlikely candidates for such glowing comparisons. One had only recently completed his formal education, while the other was still pursuing a doctorate. In trying to solve the riddle of heredity, they were locked in competition with scientists twice their age and experience, competitors who were better funded, more respected and further established. The two men even risked their own jobs when the head of the institution they worked for ordered them not to pursue their DNA model. Yet they kept working, and managed to solve one of science's most daunting riddles despite their relative youth and inexperience.

Their names are Francis Crick and James Watson. This is their story.

*Jim Watson (left) and Francis Crick immediately became good friends. Others at Cavendish Laboratory often complained that their discussions grew very loud. Eventually they were moved to their own office so they wouldn't disturb anyone.*

*Top: Jim Watson (age 11) with his father and sister Elizabeth (Betty). Bottom: Jim Watson in kindergarten at Horace Mann Elementary. He is second from left sitting on floor.*

# Chapter 2
## *Early Discoveries*

• • • • • • • • • • • • • • • • • • • • • • • • • • • • • • • • • • • • • • • •

In the 1930s and '40s, before television became popular, many American families spent their evenings gathered around another box—the radio. Then as now, they tuned in to a steady diet of comedies, dramas, news programs—and game shows. In Chicago one of the most popular game shows was "Quiz Kids." Featuring pre-teens answering questions that most adults would struggle with, it was a showcase for budding young geniuses.

In 1940, one of the contestants was a skinny 12-year-old boy with jug ears and an advanced knowledge of the sciences. While he won several times and earned a savings bond, eventually he was eliminated.

It was one of the few early disappointments in Jim Watson's life.

James Dewey Watson, Jr. was born in Chicago on April 6, 1928 to bill collector James Dewey Watson and school secretary Jean (Mitchell) Watson. Two years later a sister, Betty, joined the family.

As a youngster, Jimmy became interested in the world of science because of birds. His father was an avid birdwatcher. Even as a toddler, Jimmy tagged along on his father's various explorations. It was a chance for the two to spend time together—a precious gift as James Sr.'s job kept him very busy. However, the young boy quickly progressed beyond his father's level and became interested in everything about the birds he observed: how they flew, what they ate,

*Left: Watson at age 5; right: Watson at age 10*

the way they raised their young. This ability to focus on the tiniest details would serve him well as an adult.

The youngster's education began at the University of Chicago nursery school and continued at the Horace Mann Elementary School. Even in the lower grades, he was ahead of his peers. In a later interview, he admitted that he wasn't very popular, and had a difficult time getting along with other kids his age. He preferred the company of adults, who were more likely to share his interests in reading, serious music and science.

After eight years at Horace Mann, Jim enrolled at South Shore High School in the ninth grade. It was a brief stay.

An educator named Robert Hutchins had developed a new program designed to admit advanced high school students to the University of Chicago. Bright, but unpopular, Jim was bored in school, and often learned more outside of the classroom than in it.

He was the ideal candidate for Hutchins' program.

He was admitted in 1943 after his sophomore year in high school. By the spring of 1947, he'd earned a Bachelor of Science degree in zoology, with particular emphasis on ornithology—the study of birds.

Not yet 20, Jim's academic career had been an almost uninterrupted ascension, with few real challenges. All that changed in 1947. His first two choices for graduate study, Harvard and the California Institute of Technology, rejected him. Perhaps one reason was that throughout his undergraduate career, Jim had stubbornly refused to take any chemistry or physics courses.

"At the University of Chicago, I was principally interested in birds and managed to avoid taking any chemistry or physics classes which looked of even medium

*Watson, at age 18, at the University of Chicago. He was admitted in 1943 after his sophomore year in high school. He earned his undergraduate degree before he was 20 years old.*

difficulty," he later wrote in *The Double Helix*, his account of his momentous discovery.

But his interest in birds flew out the window when he read a book called *What is Life?* by Erwin Schrödinger during his senior year at Chicago. It described genes as the most important area of biology and argued that scientists should find out everything they could about them. Jim Watson decided this was exactly what he wanted to do.

Finally he earned a research fellowship at Indiana University in Bloomington. He was given an annual stipend, which while less than $1,000.00, would be enough to survive on. He was ready to throw himself into the study of genetics.

As young James began pursuing an advanced degree at an age when most people are just starting college, Francis Crick was in his early 30s. But despite being more than a decade older, Francis wasn't much more advanced academically than the teenager who would be his future partner. It wasn't because of laziness. It was because of a war.

Francis Harry Compton Crick was born at home in Northampton, England on June 8, 1916. His father, Harry, was a boot and shoe factory owner, while his mother Anne Elizabeth a housewife with a deep and abiding hope for her child. As Crick recalled in his autobiography, *What Mad Pursuit*, "After I was born she instructed her younger sister, Ethel, to carry me to the top of our house. My mother hoped that this little ceremony would make sure that, in later life, I would 'rise to the top.' This family legend shows rather clearly that my mother, like many another mother, was ambitious for her first-born son even before she had any inkling of my character and abilities."

His mother's hope and faith in her son would ultimately be rewarded, but it would take some time. As a child, Francis owned the natural curiosity seen in most preschoolers. While this inquisitiveness—this desire to find out how the world works—often disappears when children get older, Francis never stopped questioning the world around him.

"I think I was always interested in science... I wanted to know what is the world made of?" Francis Crick told an interviewer with the Carolina Biological Supply Company. "And because I asked so many questions, they bought me something called *Children's Encyclopedia*. And that covered all subjects. It covered history and literature and music as well as science."

For some time it was difficult to tear the child away from the books that he found so fascinating. He read what they had to say about our galaxy, about chemistry, about the atom. The books were more than a diversion. They changed his life. It wouldn't be the last time Francis's path was altered by something he read, but it was the first time he realized he wanted to be a scientist.

The decision was an exciting one, but not without a touch of melancholy. Because, as he told the Carolina Biological Company, "[I] did confide to my mother, I said 'You know by the time I grow up everything would have been discovered.' She said, 'Don't you worry! When you grow up there will be plenty for you left to discover.'"

She couldn't possibly know how true that statement would prove to be.

*Probably the most famous scientist the world has ever known, Albert Einstein waited years before his theories were accepted—or even understood! Nearly half a century later, Francis Crick and James Watson would be part of a discovery that would become as famous as Einstein's Theory of Relativity.*

# Chapter 3

## *What Is Life?*

**F**rancis Crick began his schooling at the Northampton Grammar School, and at the age of 14 he won a scholarship to Mill Hill School in North London where he became a boarding student. Then in 1934 he enrolled at the University College in London, studying physics. The study of matter, energy and the way the two interact was a fairly new discipline; Francis believed it offered a way to unlock the universe's secrets.

The dawn of the 20th century had been a great time for physics. The field was crafted by men like Max Planck, whose theories on radiation and energy were published in 1900, and Albert Einstein, who developed his theory of relativity in 1905. Einstein's theory, expressed as the famous equation $E=MC^2$, holds that energy and matter are convertible into each other. The equation would have more impact on the lives of 20th century scientists than almost any other concept.

Nearly half a century later, Francis Crick would someday be part of a discovery that would have a similar long-lasting effect.

He graduated from University College in 1937 and immediately began working toward his doctorate. Unfortunately, while Crick's studies were going well, Europe was experiencing some of the worst strife the continent had ever known. Adolf Hitler and his Nazi Party gained control of Germany in the early 1930s, and in 1939 the German army invaded Poland. England declared war on Germany, and the conflict soon became known as World War II.

The following year, Crick left school to take a job with the British Admiralty, the department which oversaw the Royal Navy. He designed underwater mines to blow up enemy shipping.

He also found time to get married, to Ruth Doreen Dodd. Their son Michael was born late in 1940.

His schooling wouldn't resume until nearly two years after the end of the war, when he enrolled at Cambridge University. By then, his marriage had fallen apart. Francis Crick was 31 years old, divorced, and still without a doctorate.

*Max Planck (left) was a theoretical physicist who developed the theory of quantum physics. Jim Watson worked under Salvador Luria (right), a biologist, who was later named one of three winners of the 1969 Nobel Prize for medicine.*

Across the Atlantic, Jim Watson had narrowed the focus of his doctorate studies. Working under Salvador Luria—a future Nobel Prize winner—he began studying what were called bacteriophages, extremely simple life forms that some geneticists believed would reveal how genes controlled cellular heredity.

Though Luria hated chemists, he believed that chemistry was necessary to study genes. But soon after beginning to study that subject, Jim almost blew up an entire chemical lab.

"I was relieved from further true chemistry," he commented in *The Double Helix*.

So in 1950 when Jim had earned his Ph.D. in Zoology from Indiana at the age of 22, Luria helped his star student to obtain a postdoctoral fellowship in Copenhagen, Denmark to study biochemistry. Studying chemistry there wasn't any better due to his boss's personal problems and heavily accented English, but it led to a seminar in Naples, Italy. It was there that Jim saw images of DNA taken by a scientist named Maurice Wilkins at King's College in London using a process known as X-ray diffraction. The images were fuzzy, and showed an odd shape completely foreign to young Jim. Still there was something about the picture, representing as it did, Jim's first view of DNA. It was a turning point in his life.

"Suddenly I was excited about chemistry," he wrote in *The Double Helix*. "Before Maurice's talk I had worried about the possibility that the gene might be fantastically irregular. Now, however, I knew that genes could crystallize; hence they must have a regular structure that could be solved in a straightforward way."

*Jim Watson at age 18 near his home in Chicago, Illinois*

Jim Watson was certain that X-ray diffraction would be the key to solving the genetic puzzle he'd read about in the book *What is Life?* He was equally certain that his time in Copenhagen was coming to an end. He asked the foundation that was funding his fellowship to transfer him to the Cavendish Laboratory at Cambridge University, where exciting work was being done under the leadership of Max Perutz and John Kendrew.

The foundation wasn't very enthusiastic and there was some doubt that they would continue to supply him with money.

To Jim, the sacrifice was worth it. He had some money saved up and he was able to rent a tiny room from one of his new bosses very inexpensively.

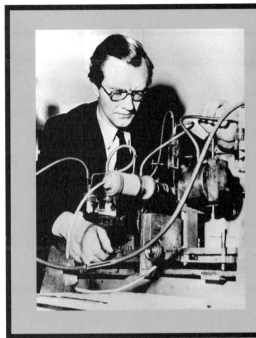

*Dr. Maurice Wilkins is shown here working in his laboratory. Dr. Wilkins was jointly awarded the 1962 Nobel Prize for Medicine with U.S. Biologist James Watson and British scientist, Francis Crick.*

So in October, 1951, James Watson left for the Cavendish Laboratory. It was where a fellow avid reader of *What is Life?* was pursuing his doctorate.

Francis Crick had been as moved by the book as Jim Watson had been, although Francis would point out later in his autobiography that "It was only later I came to see its limitations—like many physicists, he knew nothing of chemistry—but he certainly made it seem as if great things were just around the corner."

Although he was describing Erwin Schrödinger, the author of *What is Life?*, Francis Crick could just as easily have been describing young Jim Watson, who also knew little about chemistry, and also believed great things were just around the corner.

Except in Jim's case, this was true.

*Francis Crick is the co-discoverer of the structure of the DNA molecule.*

# Chapter 4

## *Strange Ways*

● ● ● ● ● ● ● ● ● ● ● ● ● ● ● ● ● ● ● ● ● ● ● ● ● ● ● ● ● ● ● ● ● ● ● ● ● ● ● ● ● ● ●

**W**hen he left the Admiralty in 1947, Francis Crick had no idea what he wanted to do. He was facing the same problem many young adults have: While he didn't know what career to pursue, he knew exactly what he *didn't* want to do. The problem was, Francis wasn't 17, he was a middle-aged doctoral student with a growing son and an ex-wife.

"By the time most scientists have reached age thirty, they are trapped by their own expertise," he recalled in his autobiography, *What Mad Pursuit.* "They have invested so much effort in one particular field that it is often extremely difficult, at that time in their careers, to make a radical change. I on the other hand, knew nothing, except for a basic training in somewhat old fashioned physics and mathematics and an ability to turn my hand to new things....Since I essentially knew nothing, I had an almost completely free choice."

Well, not exactly.

"It was so late in my career that I knew I had to make the right choice the first time," he continued. "I could hardly try one subject for two or three years and then switch to a radically different one. Whatever choice I made would be final, at least for many years."

At a loss as to what to do, he spoke to his friends. A few suggested he try writing for *Nature*, a top science publication. Crick didn't want to do that. He didn't want to report new discoveries, he wanted to make them.

It took him quite a while to realize something that many people, sadly, never figure out. By remembering his childhood dreams, what he wanted to be when he "grew up," he discovered his adult ambitions. What Crick wanted to do was scientific research, unlocking the universe's secrets. It was an area he couldn't stop talking about. He spoke about scientific discoveries the way some people talk about movies or sports.

Unfortunately when he told his friends of his ambition, most of them thought he was being ridiculous. None of them thought he was qualified to become a scientist. They told him his education was too limited, his experience useless. Finally Francis went to Georg Kreisel, a mathematician he'd trusted for some time.

"He thought for a moment," Crick later recalled in his autobiography, "and delivered his judgment. 'I've known a lot of people more stupid than you who've made a success of it.'"

That was all the motivation Crick needed. He decided then and there he would focus on a career in scientific research, but what *kind* of research? He realized what really fascinated him were the dark areas of science where earlier explanations had relied on either religion or superstition. Only in the last 50 years had genuine scientific solutions begun to be offered. Crick contemplated two areas: the brain and its workings, and molecular biology, what he called "the borderline between living and non-living."

Crick realized he was better prepared for the second area of study than the first. He'd read a number of books dealing with molecular science, and during his time at the

Admiralty he often secretly read textbooks on organic chemistry when he was supposed to be working.

As he prepared to put his energy into a career in molecular biology, the worst possible thing happened. Francis Crick was offered a job. Just a week after he made up his mind, out of the blue an entirely different solution was offered. The job would have nothing to do with his dreams. It involved studying the workings of the eye with Hamilton Hartridge, a maverick scientist who wanted to disprove a commonly accepted idea about vision.

The position promised a certain level of security and even a career path. But despite being broke, and with the financial responsibilities of a child and an ex-wife, Francis turned Hamilton down. It was a difficult decision, but Francis Crick had made up his mind and wasn't about to let something as trivial as earning a living change his mind.

Francis continued his doctoral studies at Cambridge while looking for a job to match his ambitions. It wasn't easy. At one point he tried to get hired by J.D. Bernal, an X-ray crystallographer whose work would later form the basis for studying genes. Francis couldn't get past the man's secretary. She told the aspiring scientist, "Do you realize that people from all over the world want to come work with the professor? Why do you think he would take you on?"

Finally, Francis got a chance. It came not because of his background but because a researcher at Strangeways Laboratory, a part of Cambridge University, had died, leaving an office vacant. As far as Francis was concerned, an opportunity was an opportunity and he took the job despite the odd way he earned it.

The stipend from the Medical Research Council (MRC) was quite low, so despite being well into his 30s, Francis went to his father and asked him for a loan. The work Francis embarked on was tedious, the type of research a low level scientist earning his doctorate often does. He focused primarily on cytoplasm—the inside of a cell—and after a year or so was able to get his first professional paper published. Entitled "Experimental Cell Research," it was an important step in his career. Just as important, the work he was doing left him with enough free time to do his own reading and research.

By the late 1940s, the study of DNA and genetics was gaining attention. It was an area Crick had been interested in for some time, but his first step toward pursuing it as a career came during a routine meeting with his supervisor. It was 1949, and he learned during that meeting about the MRC's creation of a new unit at the Cavendish Laboratory, also at Cambridge. Its goal was to study the structure of proteins using X-ray diffraction. The laboratory's head, Sir Lawrence Bragg, had developed the technique. His work earned him the Nobel Prize in 1915 making him, at age 25, the youngest winner ever!

X-ray diffraction analyzes the patterns created when X-rays are beamed through a crystal of a molecule being examined. By directing beams in different directions, the "diffraction pattern" is captured on photographic paper. Using these images, it's possible to determine the structure of the molecule and where the atoms line up. It was this very type of diffraction image that would one day capture Jim Watson's attention and prompt him to also join the Cavendish.

So Francis Crick moved to the Cavendish Laboratory, working under such notable scientific minds as Perutz, Kendrew and Bragg.

The job would form the basis for Francis Crick's doctoral work as his education gained the same focus his career now had. Not only did Francis know what he wanted to do, he was able to do it.

His personal life was equally satisfying. Over the previous two years he'd fallen in love with a French woman, Odile Speed, whom he'd first met during his time at the Admiralty. Back then she'd been a naval officer, but after the war, Odile focused on art and interior design. Her artistic background offered a good balance for Francis, who while creative could also be cerebral and precise. Beyond her artistic nature, his new bride was an excellent cook and entertainer.

The couple moved into a flat, or small apartment, on the upper floors of an old home in Cambridge. After a great deal of struggle, and considerable worry, Francis Crick's life seemed to be coming together. And soon, he would meet the young man who would offer him as much in his work as Odile offered him in his home.

*Although Francis Crick (left) was older, Jim Watson was better educated. Francis loved physics, Jim loved biology. The two scientists complemented each other perfectly.*

# Chapter 5

## *The Genetic Story*

J im Watson stood out at Cambridge, but then he stood out everywhere. At the University of Chicago he dressed the way most college students dress today—casually—in old shirts, beat-up pants, sneakers. But Jim was a student in the late 1940s, a time when most male students still wore jackets and ties. Besides his clothes, he had quickly gained a reputation for being difficult when he arrived at the University of Indiana, an arguer unafraid to take on the opinions of professors twice his age. His opinions made it as difficult for him to make friends as it had been in grade school. At graduate seminars, whenever he found a fellow student boring, Jim would casually open a book and start reading.

He arrived at Cambridge with all of those factors—his casual clothes, opinionated attitude, and unwillingness to listen to others if he found them boring. Still, with his American accent and crew cut at Cambridge he was something of an exotic, and mostly tolerated for his eccentricities. Some of his peers might have harshly judged the young man's behavior, but at least one person—Odile Crick—never did.

In fact, she met her husband's future partner before he did, when Perutz brought him over to the couple's flat. When she later told her husband about the meeting, Odile described Jim Watson as "an American who had no hair" after mistaking his crew cut for baldness.

Upon meeting Jim himself, Francis realized the two had a lot in common. They both had a shared fondness for *What is Life* and believed the study of genetics was the most important work a scientist could do.

Professionally the two men complemented each other quite well. Although he was considerably older, Francis Crick had only two years' experience in biology. Jim had a Ph.D. in the subject while Francis was still a doctoral student. Yet Jim had hated studying physics in school, the focus of Francis' undergraduate education. While its usefulness might not have seemed readily apparent in pursuing genetics, it offered the type of balance that two men considering partnership need. All in all, it was a good match and the two aspiring scientists became inseparable.

"From my first day in the lab I knew I would not leave Cambridge for a long time," Jim Watson recalled in *The Double Helix*. "Departing would be idiocy, for I had immediately discovered the fun of talking to Francis Crick."

At work their discussions sometimes grew so boisterous that others complained. Eventually a senior scientist had the two moved into their own office so they wouldn't disturb anyone else.

Despite the fact that Jim Watson was only in his early 20s, and Francis Crick still a doctoral student, they decided to solve the puzzle of heredity—how we become who we are. It had been puzzling scientists, and indeed many other people, for several millennia.

Around 350 B.C., the Greek philosopher Aristotle first theorized about how offspring take on the characteristics of their parents. He believed that parents passed their blood, which carried their characteristics, on to their children. This theory—which many people believed for nearly 2,000 years— is likely the origin of terms such as "blood relative" and "bloodline" (a term often applied to thoroughbred horses).

Modern genetics traces its history to the work of Gregor Mendel, an Austrian monk who was born in 1822. The child of a poor family, he wound up in a monastery and took courses at the University of Vienna, with a focus on mathematics.

It was his skill with math, not his scientific ability, which enabled him to make the first small steps in solving the inheritance riddle with a series of experiments he began in 1856 and continued for seven years. He chose the common garden pea, a far simpler subject than a human being but a good first choice for the study of inherited traits. He selected peas from a variety of pods—long and short, green and yellow—which came from two types of seeds: wrinkled and

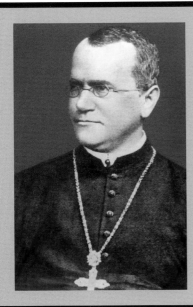

*Gregor Mendel was an Austrian monk who studied the garden pea when he noticed that sometimes a pea would have qualities not seen in the pea it came from directly. He determined that each pea plant owned several pairs of elements that controlled a trait in a plant. He is credited with discovering the foundation of heredity. Many scientists took Mendel's work much further, including Barbara McClintock, Oswald Avery, and Wilhelm Johannsen.*

round. By cross-pollinating—transferring pollen from one plant to another—he was able to breed plants that *bred true* so a specific trait appeared. But with each generation of pea, he noticed that often a pea would have qualities not seen in the pea it came from directly, but that had been present in earlier generations. Some plants grown from round seeds would have offspring that bore wrinkled seeds, some green pea pods produced yellow pea pods.

Gregor Mendel determined that each pea plant owned several pairs of elements, or what we now call genes. Each of these elements controlled a trait in the plant—whether it was yellow or green, long or short. Each element could be strong or weak; the strong element we would now call a "dominant gene" and the weak element we now refer to as a "recessive gene."

Using a complex mathematical formula, he was able to craft heredity laws, most of which were eventually proven true. In those laws, plants that inherited two strong traits would have the strong trait. In other words, if the trait for a green plant was dominant, then its offspring would be green. If a plant inherited the strong trait and the weak trait, it would still have the strong trait. Mendel noticed that these genes are inherited independently, so the plant can inherit one gene without the other. This is why traits can appear that are not seen in the parents. It is why yellow pea pods can have green pea-podded offspring.

His reward for all this painstaking effort? Total obscurity.

In his lifetime, few scientists read his papers or attended his lectures. His only published article covering his research, "Experiments with Plant Hybrids," appeared in 1865 in a scientific journal with little respect and few readers. When Mendel died in 1884, few scientists even knew who he was.

Fifteen years after Mendel's death, a series of experiments by Hugo de Vries, Carl Correns and Erich Tschermak utilizing Mendel's papers proved many of his theories.

And as the 20th century dawned, the study of genetics gained respectability. Two reasons were especially important. One was the immense improvement in microscopes, which finally allowed scientists to peer inside the nucleus of individual cells. The other was what they found: long thin rod-like structures that became colored when they were treated with certain stains to make them more visible. They were called "chromosomes," from two Greek words which mean literally "colored bodies." Chromosomes, scientists quickly realized, were responsible for the transmission of

*Three scientists in three countries—Hugo de Vries of Holland (shown here), Karl Correns of Germany, and Erich von Tschermak of Austria—all tried to determine the laws of heredity by doing experiments with plants. All three came to essentially the same conclusion at about the same time, in the year 1900. But when they got ready to publish their findings, they discovered that Gregor Mendel had discovered the laws of genetics three decades before and his journal had gone unnoticed in that time. Mendel died in 1884.*

hereditary characteristics from one generation to the next, and each chromosome—human beings have 46—contain scores or even thousands of individual traits that soon became known as genes.

In *What Mad Pursuit*, Francis Crick points out, "Genetics tells us that, roughly speaking, we get half of all our genes from our mother, in the egg, and the other half from our father, in the sperm." Since a single sperm is too small to be seen without a microscope, it stands to reason genes must be quite small as well. "Yet in this small space," explains Crick, "must be housed an almost complete set of instructions for building an entire human being (the egg providing the duplicate set.)"

These genes are no larger than a very large molecule, what is called a macromolecule. While this awareness doesn't explain the gene's functions, it does, as Crick notes, make it necessary to study their chemistry. In 1897, Eduard Buchner discovered enzymes, which are needed for these macromolecules to undergo the rapid chemical reaction— or catalyst—in order to change.

In 1926, American chemist James Summer proved these enzymes were all part of the same macromolecule family called proteins. In the 1930s, George Beadle and Ed Tatum put forth the next important postulate in their "one gene - one enzyme" theory. As Crick points out, "... the general plan of living things seems almost obvious. Each gene determines a particular protein. Some of these proteins are used to form structures or carry signal, while many of them are the catalysts that decide what chemical reactions should and should not take place in each cell. Almost every cell in our bodies has a complete set of genes within it, and

*In the 1930s, Dr. George Beadle (left) and Dr. Edward Tatum (right) developed their "one gene-one enzyme" theory while working together at Stanford University. The men later shared the 1958 Nobel Prize for medicine for their work in establishing what genes do. They shared this prize with Joshua Lederberg.*

this chemical program directs how each cell metabolizes, grows and interacts with its neighbors."

But what was in each gene that carried this chemical program? For years, scientists were bitterly divided. Many favored proteins, while a minority were on the side of DNA.

In the 1940s, research relating to DNA had begun in earnest. In New York, the Rockefeller Institute's Oswald Avery conducted a series of experiments using mice in order to discover the so-called "transforming factor" that changed harmless pneumococci bacteria into deadly pneumococci bacteria. He later conducted tests that identified the transforming factor. It was the gene streptococcus, and it was made of DNA!

Privately Oswald Avery wrote to his brother that the experiment proved the nucleic acid in DNA was "not merely structurally important but functionally active substances in determining the biochemical activities and specific characteristics of cells."

*Oswald Avery, shown here, discovered in the 1940s that DNA was genetic material. He worked at the Rockefeller Institute Hospital (now Rockefeller University) with Colin MacLeod and Maclyn McCarty. Up until that time, scientists did not know what DNA was.*

In other words, DNA wasn't just some "stupid substance" as many of Avery's colleagues believed. It did something—it was important. Unfortunately, Avery kept most of his theories to himself, and in his sole published paper on the matter, he didn't make a very compelling argument. Avery died as Mendel had, with few of his peers believing him.

However, one scientist at Columbia University did see the value in Avery's work. Erwin Chargaff didn't just repeat Avery's experiments, but took them one step forward. Utilizing a technique called paper chromatography, the scientist examined the four DNA chemical bases: adenine, thymine, guanine and cytosine. In his paper on the work, Chargaff noted how in every species he examined the proportions of the four bases were different, but they were always present. He also noted that in every species he examined, the percentages of adenine and thymine were virtually identical. The same held true for guanine and cytosine. Almost as an afterthought, he noted he couldn't find any differences in the DNA he examined from the nuclei of regular cells versus those he took from sperm. This linked DNA to everything from hair to skin to internal organs.

The discovery only added to DNA's significance.

So as the 1950's began, it was clear that DNA was vital to understanding the secrets of genetics. But one mystery remained: What was the actual chemical structure of DNA that enabled it to perform its vital hereditary function? Francis Crick and Jim Watson wanted to find out. But they were not the only ones.

*In 1951, Barbara McClintock, working at Cold Spring Harbor Laboratory discovered that genes do not always remain stationary. Working with corn plants, she found what scientists called transposable elements and journalists like to call "jumping genes."*

# Chapter 6
## *The Secret Of Life*

· · · · · · · · · · · · · · · · · · · · · · · · · · · · · · · · · · · · · · · · · · ·

**A**long the fringes of Cambridge University's Cavendish Laboratory, a low-slung building in some disrepair stood out from the rest of the school. It would serve as the home for Watson and Crick's research. Among the other scientists it was known as "The Hut." But its untidy appearance was in contrast to the incredible work going on inside its walls.

As *Current Biography 1963* described it, "A casual visitor, glancing inside The Hut, would hardly have recognized it as a scientific laboratory, much less the birthplace of one of biology's most fruitful concepts. Here, among a welter of old books, Watson and Crick began putting together an elaborate three-dimensional jigsaw puzzle, out of pieces of wire and colored beads and steel rods and oblongs of sheet metal. They sought a model of the deoxyribonucleic acid (DNA) molecule that would fit all the known facts and that might yield a molecular explanation of how living matter reproduces itself."

They already knew that DNA was a complex chemical compound formed of several types of compounds—sugars, phosphates and bases. But with just one doctorate between them and less than a combined decade's worth of experience as researchers, Francis Crick and Jim Watson had their work cut out for them. In addition, trying to determine the structure of DNA wasn't even their primary responsibility at Cavendish.

But it was for two scientists at nearby King's College. One was Wilkins, whose work had already fired Jim's imagination. The other was Rosalind Franklin. Unfortunately she had two hurdles to overcome: DNA's complexity and her gender. At King's College, her first job was working with Wilkins using X-ray diffraction to uncover DNA's structure.

"Almost from the moment she arrived in Maurice's lab," Watson later described in *The Double Helix*, "they began to upset each other. Maurice, a beginner in X-ray diffraction work wanted some professional help and hoped that Rosy, a trained crystallographer, could speed up the research. Rosy, however, did not see the situation this way. She claimed she had been given DNA for her own problem and would not think of herself as Maurice's assistant."

Some felt the conflict was due to Wilkins' inability to accept a bright woman's opinions. He wasn't alone. Because

*Rosalind Franklin, an associate of Maurice Wilkins, used X-ray crystallography to develop the idea of the double helix. She presented her idea in 1951 at a talk at Cambridge which Watson attended. Watson does not remember or accept this. Franklin died tragically of cancer in 1958 at the age of 37. Had she lived, it is likely she would have shared in the Nobel Prize with Crick, Watson, and Wilkins. During her lifetime, however, there was a lot of animosity between Franklin and Wilkins and between Franklin and Watson, most of which can be attributed to the attitude in the science community at the time which held that women scientists were merely assistants, and not capable of being equal to male scientists.*

of her gender, Franklin was barred from the faculty dining room and found her point of view consistently ignored.

Despite the drama, Rosalind Franklin's contributions were important because the images she created were the closest anyone came to showing the structure of DNA. Because of her talent as a crystallographer she was able to provide a clear enough view of DNA to provide a valuable starting point for other scientists, one of whom was Jim Watson. He often sat in on her seminars.

During her time at King's College, Franklin was satisfied with recording the measurements taken from diffraction plates. Watson and Crick wanted to do more.

They wanted to build a solid model of DNA—a three-dimensional construction. Using Wilkins' and Franklin's diffraction images was like building a puzzle with half the pieces missing because there were angles that they needed that a two-dimensional image would not provide.

Constructing a model of DNA quickly turned into a dilemma that combined Jim Watson's youth with Francis Crick's inexperience. Jim Watson was so eager to get started on the project that when he reported back to Francis Crick, he often left out some of the most important details from Rosalind's presentations. Relying on only partial information, Crick's first attempts to build a model of DNA were laughably bad. In fact, when the two men invited Rosalind Franklin to view their work, she complained it was completely inaccurate and the two inexperienced scientists were wasting her time.

Worse still, word of the two men's ill-advised model of DNA quickly got back to Bragg. He was furious. Neither man was authorized to work on DNA modeling. Bragg believed if two British research teams were competing to find DNA's structure, government funding from the MRC might be eliminated. After all, neither Watson nor Crick were as experienced as Wilkins and Franklin, so how could the two men do anything other than duplicate what was being done at King's College, and badly at that?

It was just before Christmas 1951 when Bragg angrily ordered Crick to return to his protein research, and Watson to get back to his study of the tobacco mosaic virus.

Of course, Francis Crick and Jim Watson had already overcome educational and financial obstacles. They weren't about to let a supervisor's orders get in their way. They decided to continue working on their DNA model. They just wouldn't tell anyone about it.

They were also competing with Linus Pauling, a California Institute of Technology chemistry professor, who was also studying DNA and would later become world

Crick and Watson knew they were in a race with other scientists to map the structure of the DNA molecule. Most believed that the race was between Watson-Crick working at Cambridge University and Linus Pauling (shown here) and Robert B. Corey working at the California Institute of Technology. Pauling and Corey had found that many proteins were shaped like a coil, or helix and they believed that DNA had a similar structure.

famous for his tireless promotion of Vitamin C as a cure for many diseases. In 1948, he drew a flat chain diagram of DNA. But he realized that the structure wouldn't work and then imagined it as a long spiraling coil, or helix. Three years later, his published paper on this helix was another important step in the DNA race.

For Watson and Crick, Pauling's helix model was encouraging. However, both men knew it was not completely accurate. They just weren't sure why. It was Linus Pauling's son, Peter, who showed the two men his father's calculations.

"At once I felt that something was not right," Jim Watson would later recall in *The Double Helix*. After careful checking, he realized that Pauling had made a mistake with his phosphate groups calculations. The DNA "chain" would surely fall apart. The error wasn't great news; Watson realized all it did was buy them some time.

At this point Rosalind Franklin inadvertently helped the two men out. All along she'd refused to consider their theories about DNA's structure, but while earlier images she'd made had hinted at the double helix of DNA, her latest images proved it. They couldn't have come at a better time, arriving as they did when Francis and Jim were head to head with Linus Pauling. As soon as Jim Watson left Rosalind Franklin's lecture, he knew what he needed to do. "A potential key to the secret of life was impossible to push out of my mind," he later wrote. "It was certainly better to imagine myself becoming famous then maturing into a stifled academic who never risked a thought."

On the train from London to Cambridge, Jim furiously sketched his new idea for the DNA helix that showed two interwoven strands. Back in Cambridge he and Francis determined that each base (adenine, thymine, guanine and cytosine) was connected to a complementary base. In other words, adenine hooked up with thymine, guanine with cytosine—what Chargaff's research had hinted at three years earlier.

The Cold Spring Harbor web site explains this discovery by saying, "Because each nucleotide (base) within a rung of the DNA ladder is always paired with the same complementary nucleotide, one half of the molecule can serve as a template for the construction of the other half. This complementary pairing explains how identical copies of parental DNA can be passed on to two daughter cells. During cell division, the DNA helix 'unzips,' and two new molecules are formed from the half ladder templates."

It was Francis Crick who first suggested that the acidic phosphate groups should be on the outside of the strand. His previous models, at Jim's insistence, had placed them inside. In *What Mad Pursuit*, he recalls the conversation. "'Why not,' I said to Jim one evening, "build models with the phosphates on the outside?' 'Because,' he said, 'that would be too easy' (meaning that there were too many models he could build in this way). 'Then why not try it?' I said."

By putting the phosphates on the outside, the bases were placed inside, which forced Crick and Watson to pay more attention to their shape and position. By this time it was early 1953, as much of Crick's time in 1952 had been spent working on his doctoral thesis, which dealt mainly with proteins. But one important piece of news had arrived while Crick was devoting his energy to his thesis: experiments by American researchers Alfred Hershey and

Martha Chase, building on Oswald Avery's research, had proven conclusively that DNA was what controlled heredity.

The two realized how little time they had before someone else solved the riddle. From a nearby machine shop, sheets of metal were produced in the shape of the bases. Carefully the two men built the model. It was tedious, time-consuming work, but a little more than one month after they started they were done.

It was in the shape of a double helix, or a ladder that continually twisted around itself. The sugar and phosphate molecules formed the "upright" sections of the ladder, while the four bases—in pairs—formed the "rungs."

They spent several days carefully checking their calculations, and unveiled their model on March 7, 1953. No one laughed or criticized them this time.

On April 25, 1953, Jim Watson and Francis Crick published the first of four papers in the prestigious scientific journal *Nature* (which just a few years previously some of Crick's friends had suggested he work for) that announced their discovery to the world. Entitled "Molecular Structure of Nucleic Acids," it was only 900 words long and included what may be one of the biggest understatements in the entire history of scientific writing: "It has not escaped our notice that the specific pairing we have postulated immediately suggests a possible copying mechanism for the genetic material."

While there was some skepticism, comments such as "unlocking the secret of life" were fairly common. The riddle of heredity had been answered. The only question was how the information would be used.

*Two photographs taken in Stockholm, Sweden at the 1962 Nobel Prize ceremony. Top, left to right: Maurice Wilkins, Max Perutz, Francis Crick, John Steinbeck, James Watson, and John Kendrew. The bottom photo was taken of these men after the ceremony.*

# Chapter 7
## *On to the Future*

• • • • • • • • • • • • • • • • • • • • • • • • • • • • • • • • • • • • • •

**I**t makes perfect sense. In order to discover the way something works, it's important to know what it looks like. With something as minuscule as DNA, this was a difficult task. By building a working model of DNA's double helix, Francis Crick and Jim Watson offered guidance to the generations of scientists who followed them.

Francis Crick finally earned his doctorate in 1954. Eight years later, in 1962 he would share the Nobel Prize in Physiology or Medicine with his partner Watson, and Maurice Wilkins, whose X-ray diffraction work led the way to the model. Rosalind Franklin's contribution was barely noted. But she had died in 1958 at the age of 37, and Nobel Prize rules do not allow posthumous awards. Crick, for one, believes that she would have been included if she had still been alive.

By then the two partners had gone their separate ways. Francis Crick remained in England until 1976 when he left for the Salk Institute for Biological Studies in La Jolla, California to pursue his interest in the brain, his other source of fascination when he made his fateful career choice nearly 30 years earlier.

Jim Watson left England to join the faculty of Harvard University in 1955. In 1968 he became director of the Cold Spring Harbor Laboratory in New York. He also became the director of the Human Genome project in 1988. Although he resigned in 1992, the quest to map the human genome—

discover the precise molecular structure of the estimated 30,000+ genes that comprise a human being—continues. Described by the UCLA Chancellor Albert Carnesale as "the set of coded instructions in our DNA," this work could lead to a variety of results. As he notes, it is a "monumental achievement, comparable in significance to the splitting of the atom. It is revolutionizing the life sciences and medicine... Knowing the code of the human genome opens the door to understanding the genetic basis of disease and tackling it accordingly."

Despite many advances, the science of genetics often generates enormous controversy. In 1974, geneticists enacted a self-imposed temporary ban on their experiments, saying in a statement that "our concern is based on judgments of potential rather than demonstrated risk since

*James Watson (left) is shown here with Barbara McClintock, Arnold Beckman, and Alfred Hershey at the dedication of the Beckman Laboratory at the Cold Spring Harbor Laboratory in New York. Arnold Beckman donated the money to build the new lab.*

there are few available experimental data on the hazards of such DNA molecules."

While the ban was lifted, controversy and questions remained. Genetics could lead to everything from cancer cures to understanding why some people are alcoholic, but it also has a great deal of risk. Issues such as cloning—making identical copies of an organism (even a human) without sexual reproduction—have been a concern since the 1970's. Recently a variety of animals have been successfully cloned, and some scientists have even claimed the ability to clone a human embryo.

These experiments have made many people very nervous. As the Council for Responsible Genetics pointed out in a 1992 letter to the Food and Drug Administration,

*From left to right: Jim Watson with wife, Elizabeth, Lita Hazen and Francis Crick*

"Those in the scientific community would do well to remember that, though Frankenstein was, in fact, the scientist, virtually everyone thinks it is the name of the monster."

Despite those fears, most in the scientific community are excited about the range of possibilities available in research. The 21st century promises to yield discoveries that couldn't have been imagined only a few years ago.

Over the years, Jim Watson and Francis Crick have continued to be honored for their contributions to science. In 1991, Crick was appointed to the Order of Merit, an honorary British institution founded in 1902 by King Edward VII to reward especially eminent service. It is limited to just 24 members. And in 2002, Watson received an honorary knighthood from England's Queen Elizabeth II.

*Crick and Watson with a re-creation of their double helix DNA model forty years later (approximately 1993).*

# Chronology of James Dewey Watson

| | |
|---|---|
| **1928** | born in Chicago, Illinois to James Watson and Jean Mitchell Watson |
| **1940** | appears on Chicago radio program "Quiz Kids" |
| **1943** | enters University of Chicago under an experimental program for teenagers |
| **1947** | earns Bachelor of Science degree in Biology |
| **1950** | receives Ph.D. in Zoology from University of Indiana |
| **1950** | begins work in Copenhagen, studying viruses and DNA |
| **1951** | at a symposium in Naples, Italy sees X-ray diffraction pattern of crystalline DNA |
| **1951** | starts work at Cavendish Laboratory in Cambridge; begins collaboration with Francis Crick |
| **1953** | publishes first paper on DNA structure with Crick |
| **1956** | joins faculty of Harvard University as assistant professor of biology |
| **1961** | becomes full professor at Harvard |
| **1962** | shares Nobel prize with Crick and Maurice Wilkins |
| **1968** | publishes controversial autobiography *The Double Helix* |
| **1968** | becomes director of Cold Spring Harbor Laboratory on Long Island, New York |
| **1988** | named head of United States Human Genome project |
| **2002** | knighted by Queen Elizabeth II |

# Chronology of Francis Harry Compton Crick

| | |
|---|---|
| **1916** | born June 8 in Northampton, England |
| **1937** | earns Bachelor of Science degree in physics from the University of London |
| **1940** | marries Ruth Doreen Dodd |
| **1940** | first son, Michael, is born |
| **1947** | divorces Ruth |
| **1947** | begins Ph.D. work at Strangeways Laboratory in Cambridge |
| **1949** | joins Medical Research Unit at Cavendish Laboratory |
| **1949** | marries Odile Speed |
| **1953** | publishes first paper on DNA structure with Watson |
| **1954** | receives Ph.D. degree |
| **1962** | shares Nobel prize with Crick and Maurice Wilkins |
| **1976** | joins the Salk Institute in La Jolla, California |
| **1991** | appointed to Order of the Merit |

# Genetics Timeline

**ca 350 BC**   Aristotle proposes that parents pass on characteristics to their children through their blood

**1595**   Zacharias Jansen invents microscope

**1665**   Robert Hooke improves Jansen's invention and describes the tiny organisms he studies as "cells" after the tiny rooms that monks lived in

**1791**   Massachusetts farmer Seth Wright breeds short-legged sheep to keep them from escaping over his fences, becoming the first to breed animals for future results

**1859**   Charles Darwin's *Origin of the Species* proposes natural selection

**1866**   Gregor Mendel publishes paper on his experiments with plant hybrids Poorly regarded at the time, it will go on to form the basis for modern genetics

**1868**   working with discarded bandages, Friedrich Miescher discovers DNA

**1890s**   August Weismann's experiments with mice proves heredity is carried through sex cells, and isn't affected by what happens after birth

**1897**   Eduard Buchner discovers enzymes

**1899**   utilizing Mendel's papers, a series of experiments by Hugo de Vries, Carl Correns and Erich Tschermak proved many of Mendel's theories

**1902**   Walter Sutton proves that chromosomes carry the cells' units of inheritance

**1909**   Wilhelm Johannsen introduces term "gene" from Greek word meaning "to give birth to."

**1915**   Thomas Hunt Morgan publishes the first map of chromosomes

**1920s**   Hermann Muller conducts experiments irradiating fruit flies, proving that mutations are the result of chemical reactions

**1926**   American chemist James Summer proves enzymes are part of the protein family

**1940**   George Beadle and Ed Tatum put forth "one gene = one enzyme" hypothesis

**1944**   Oswald Avery demonstrates that DNA carries cell's genetic information

**1947**   Barbara McClintock discovers "jumping genes," genes which move around on the chromosome.

**1950**   Erwin Chargaff publishes his paper on the four DNA bases

**1950s**   King's College scientists Maurice Wilkins and Rosalind Franklin use X-ray crystallography to determine the structure of DNA

**1952**   Alfred Hershey and Martha Chase demonstrate conclusively that DNA, not proteins, contain genetic information

**1953**   James Watson and Francis Crick publish the first of four papers in *Nature*, describing the structure of DNA

**1972** The first recombinant DNA molecules are produced; transposable elements are discovered in bacteria

**1977** Genentech, the first genetic engineering company is founded; it manufactures medical drugs

**1982** Recombinant DNA technology is used to synthesize human insulin in bacteria

**1990** Gene therapy is first used in humans; the Human Genome Project is begun coordinated by the Department of Energy and the National Institutes of Health with the goal of sequencing and mapping all genetic information

**2000** a working draft of the entire human genome sequence completed in June

**2001** analyses of the human genome sequence published in February

**2003** expected completion date of the U.S. Human Genome Project

# Further Reading

Baldwin, Joyce. *DNA Pioneer: James Watson and the Double Helix.* Walker and Company: New York, 1994.

Bryan, Jenny. *Genetic Engineering.* Thompson Learning: New York, 1995.

Crick, Francis. *What Mad Pursuit.* Basic Books: New York, 1988.

Edelson, Edward. *Francis Crick and James Watson and the Building Blocks of Life.* Oxford University Press: New York, 1998.

Gallant, Roy A. *The Origins of Life.* Benchmark Books, Marshall Cavendish: Tarrytown, NY, 2001.

Roca, Nuria and Marta Serrano. *Cells, Genes, and Chromosomes.* Chelsea House Publishers: Philadelphia, 1996.

Sherrow, Victoria. *James Watson and Francis Crick: Decoding the Secrets of DNA.* Blackbirch Press: Woodbridge, CT, 1995.

Strathern, Paul. *The Big Idea: Crick, Watson and DNA.* Doubleday: New York, 1997.

Watson, James. *The Double Helix: A Personal Account of the Discovery of the Structure of DNA.* New York: Athenum, 1968.

## On the Web

http://www.encarta.msn.com

http://www.nobel.se/medicine/laureates/1962

http://www.emuseum.mnsu

http://www.encyclopedia.com

http://www.pbs.org/wgbh

http://www.salk.edu

http://www.Time.com

# Glossary of Terms

**adenine:** one of four chemical bases of DNA

**biology:** study of living beings

**cell:** The smallest living part of any living organism

**chromosome:** long thin rod-like structures found in nucleus of all living things that are made of DNA and are responsible for transmission of hereditary characteristics

**cytosine:** one of four chemical bases of DNA

**deoxyribonucleic acid (DNA):** double helix structure that contains a cell's genetic information and is found in the nuclei of the cells of plants and animals

**enzyme:** protein that speeds up chemical reactions in the body

**gene:** part of a chromosome that carries instructions for making a protein

**genome:** complete set of nucleic acids that contain all of an organism's genetic information

**guanine:** one of four chemical bases of DNA

**helix:** an object that has a spiral shape

**molecule:** The tiniest part of either an element or a compound which still has the same physical and chemical qualities

**nucleic acid:** complex chemical compound found in cell nucleus that contains inherited traits; complex compounds that form DNA and RNA

**nucleotide:** chemical compound that is one of the building blocks of a nucleic acid

**nucleus:** center of a cell, containing the cell's basic genetic information

**mutation:** change occurring in an individual that may or may not be passed along to its offspring

**protein:** one of the many complex molecules composed of amino acids; necessary to form muscles, organs, and tissues, as well as antibodies and enzymes

**thymine:** one of four chemical bases of DNA

**X-ray diffraction:** analysis of the patterns created when X-rays are beamed through a crystal of a molecule being examined

**zoology:** branch of biology that studies animals

# Index